POINT OF IMPACT

The Moon Landing

The Race into Space

NIGEL KELLY

Heinemann Library
Chicago, Illinois

Designed by Robert Sydenham, Ambassador Design, Bristol
Originated by Ambassador Litho, Bristol.
Printed in Hong Kong

05 04 03 02 01
10 9 8 7 6 5 4 3 2 1

Library of Congress Cataloging-in-Publication Data
Kelly, Nigel.
    The moon landing : the race into space / Nigel Kelly.
        p. cm. -- (Point of impact)
    Includes bibliographical references and index.
    ISBN 1-57572-415-4 (library binding)
    1. Project Apollo (U.S.)--Juvenile literature. 2. Space flight to the
moon--History--Juvenile literature. 3. Space race--United States--Juvenile literature. [1.
Project Apollo (U.S.) 2. Space flight to the moon. 3. Space race.] I. Title. II. Series.

    TL789.8 . U6A5392 2000
    629.45'4'0973--dc21

                                                        00-059710

Acknowledgments
The Publishers would like to thank the following for permission to reproduce photographs:
Gareth Boden, p. 27; Corbis, pp. 9, 16, 17, 18; pp. 6, 10, 14 (Bettman), p. 23 (NASA), p. 11
(Roger Ressmeyer); Fortean Picture Library, p. 13; Mary Evans Picture Library, p. 12; NASA, pp. 5,
7, 23, 24; pp. 15, 19, 22 (Science Photo Library); Photodisc, p 4; Science & Society Picture
Library, p. 8; Space Imaging Inc, p. 25; Tony Stone Images, p. 29.

Cover photograph reproduced with permission of NASA (Corbis).

Our thanks to Christopher Gibb for his help in the preparation of this book.

Every effort has been made to contact copyright holders of any material reproduced in this book.
Any omissions will be rectified in subsequent printings if notice is given to the Publisher.

Some words are shown in bold, **like this.** You can find out what they mean by looking in the glossary.

Contents

The Moon Landing

One small step

At 9:32 A.M. on July 16, 1969, the *Apollo 11* mission began an epic journey from the Kennedy Space Center in Florida. In about eleven minutes, the spacecraft pushed free of Earth's **gravity** and went into **orbit.** It circled Earth one and a half times before its powerful thrusters burst into life and sent it out of orbit and across space. The three astronauts on board *Apollo 11* were Michael Collins, Neil Armstrong, and Edwin "Buzz" Aldrin. They had a mission that no one had ever been given before. They were to cross about 240,000 miles (386,000 kilometers) of space and land on Earth's moon.

Four days later, on July 20, Armstrong and Aldrin climbed into the **lunar module,** *Eagle.* It separated from the **command module,** *Columbia,* and began its journey toward the Moon's surface. Just before 4:18 P.M. came the message, "The *Eagle* has landed." For the first time, there were people on the Moon.

People have wondered about the Moon ever since they first walked on Earth. Finally, in 1969, two men had the thrill of crossing space and walking on its surface.

One giant leap

More than six hours later, Armstrong—and later, Aldrin—emerged from the lunar module. As over 600 million people watched on their television sets back on Earth, Armstrong became the first man to walk on the Moon. After taking his first step, he declared:

"That's one small step for [a] man, one giant leap for mankind."

The U.S. president, Richard Nixon, was so impressed by what Armstrong and Aldrin had done that he sent them a message saying,

"…because of what you have done, the heavens have become a part of man's world."

The astronauts had several tasks to perform during their short stay on the Moon. They collected nearly 50 pounds (23 kilograms) of soil samples to take back to Earth, set up a solar wind experiment and, of course, took many photographs as souvenirs! They also erected a United States flag. After spending two hours and 31 minutes on the Moon, the astronauts returned to the lunar module to prepare to return to *Columbia.*

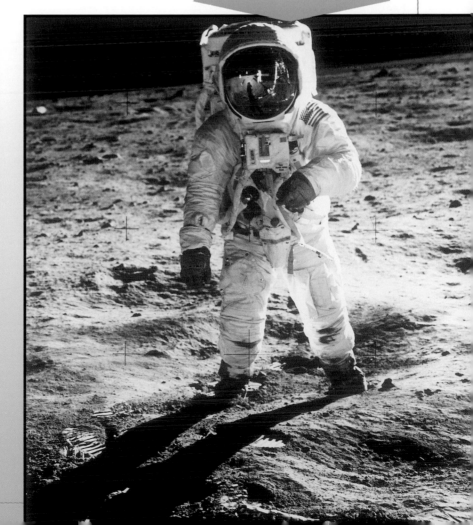

Buzz Aldrin walks on the Moon. The lunar module and Neil Armstrong are reflected in Aldrin's visor.

Apollo 11— We're Coming Home

Once they were back inside the **lunar module,** Armstrong and Aldrin removed their spacesuits and rested for several hours in preparation for their trip. Then came the heart-stopping moment when it was time to lift off and rejoin the **command module.** Fortunately, it went smoothly, and the astronauts were soon reunited with *Columbia,* orbiting the Moon. The return journey took four days, with the astronauts finally splashing down in the sea about 825 miles (1,530 kilometers) from Hawaii on July 24.

A turning point?

In 1969, the *Apollo 11* mission caused great excitement. Scientists declared that we had entered a new era in space exploration. The last great barrier in exploration had been broken down. We were now "in space," and there was no looking back. But things have not worked out quite as the scientists expected. A few more people have visited the Moon, but none in the last 30 years. The dream of having colonies of people living on the Moon or in space cities has remained just a dream. Perhaps these dreams will be realized in this new century, and the next turning point in space exploration will be reached.

The Moon landing made front-page headlines in newspapers in the United States and all over the world.

What if it had gone wrong?

We now know that if the lunar module had failed to take off to rejoin *Columbia,* Armstrong and Aldrin would have been left on the Moon, either to die slowly or to commit suicide. A plan was made in which President Richard Nixon would call the men's wives to express his condolences before going on television to inform the world that "There is a corner of another world that is forever mankind."

Neil Armstrong was the first man to set foot on the Moon.

NEIL ARMSTRONG—FIRST MAN ON THE MOON

Neil Armstrong was born in Wapakoneta, Ohio, in 1930. Beginning in 1949, he served as a pilot in the U.S. Navy, and he fought in the Korean War (1950–53). He later became a test pilot and joined the astronaut training program in 1962. His first flight into space was in 1966, when he was command pilot on *Gemini 8*. Although his became one of the most famous names in history when he walked on the Moon, he did not stay in the space program. From 1971–79, he was a professor of aerospace engineering at the University of Cincinnati, and after that, he began a career in business.

From Balloons to Rockets

The dream of flight

The *Apollo 11* mission had taken men to the Moon and back. But the idea that humans could fly had been no more than a dream until the late eighteenth century.

Hot-air balloons

In September 1783, French brothers Joseph and Étienne Montgolfier launched a balloon powered by hot air, which was created by burning straw, wool, old shoes, and rotting meat. The smell was terrible, but there were no complaints from the balloon's passengers—a sheep, a duck, and a rooster. All three survived the experience, and manned flights soon became common.

The Montgolfiers' hot-air balloon took people into the air for the first time on November 21, 1783.

Enter the airplane

The real breakthrough in flight technology came in 1903, near Kitty Hawk, North Carolina. Brothers Wilbur and Orville Wright succeeded in flying an airplane with a gas-driven engine. The first flight lasted just 12 seconds, but the age of flight had truly begun. One of the most important advances came when Sir Frank Whittle invented the **jet engine,** first used to fly a plane in 1941. Aircraft could now travel at much greater speeds. In 1952, the world's first jetliner, the British *De Haviland Comet*, went into service. It could travel at speeds of up to 500 miles per hour (800 kilometers per hour.)

War in the air

The first use to which people put this exciting new technology was to help them fight wars. A few aircraft carried out bombing raids during World War I. By World War II, aircraft bombers were used with devastating effectiveness. On August 6, 1945, the first **atomic bomb** was dropped from an American B-29 bomber on the Japanese city of Hiroshima. It killed as many as 80,000 men, women, and children outright, and many more died later from radiation sickness caused by the bomb.

Rocket technology

Meanwhile, scientists were developing the technology that would make war in the air even more deadly. In 1926, Robert Goddard, an American scientist, built the first effective **rocket.** By 1939, German rocket engineer Wernher von Braun had succeeded in developing rockets that could replace the German flying bombs. These V-2 rockets could reach an altitude of 50 miles (80 kilometers) before falling and exploding. Before long, it was possible for rockets to travel fast enough to escape the pull of Earth's **gravity** and travel into space!

This intercontinental ballistic missile was launched from a nuclear-powered submarine by the United States Navy as part of a demonstration during the Cold War.

The Cold War

After World War II, a **Cold War** developed between the Western countries, led by the United States, and the countries of Eastern Europe, led by the **Soviet Union.** The West was **democratic,** while the East was **communist.** Each side was determined to prove that its system was best. The two sides spent huge sums of money building up supplies of weapons, although no direct fighting actually took place. Both sides used rocket technology to develop weapons. **ICBMs (intercontinental ballistic missiles)** were rockets with **nuclear bombs** attached that could hit targets several thousand miles away.

The Final Frontier— Into the Unknown

The space race

The desire to win the **Cold War** pushed both the United States and the **Soviet Union** to develop the technology to send **rockets** into space. What better way could there be to prove the superiority of a country than to be first to put a man in space—or better still, on the Moon? So from the mid–1950s, the two **superpowers** took part in a "space race." Winning this race would show how much more advanced the victor's science and technology were than those of their rivals.

The race begins

In August 1957, Soviet scientists developed a rocket to power their **ICBMs.** The same type of rocket was used to send a **satellite** into space on October 4, 1957. *Sputnik 1* was a tiny sphere, housing two radio transmitters, but its successful **orbit** of Earth marked the beginning of the space age. In November 1957, the larger *Sputnik 2* carried a dog, Laika, into space. She died of heat exhaustion before her air ran out.

Wernher von Braun was a rocket engineer who played an important part in developing rockets used in space exploration.

The success of the *Sputnik* launches made the United States even more determined to launch its own rockets. The first attempt, in December 1957, ended in failure, when the launch rocket exploded shortly after lift-off. In January 1958, however, they were successful when *Explorer 1* was launched into space by a *Jupiter* rocket—developed by Wernher von Braun, who had been brought to the United States after World War II.

In 1959, the United States sent monkeys into space. In contrast to the *Sputnik 2* mission, the animals were brought safely back to Earth. The technology existed to send animals into space and bring them back. Now it was time to do it with humans.

Miss Baker was one of the "monkeynauts" sent into space by the United States in 1959.

WERNHER VON BRAUN (1912–77)

Wernher von Braun came from a wealthy German family. He became interested in astronomy when his mother gave him a telescope as a present. It is said that he did badly in math and physics at school until he was given a copy of a book about rockets. He was so annoyed that he could not understand it that he began to work really hard.

In 1930, he joined the German Society for Space Travel, and by 1934 had helped develop a rocket that could reach a height of 1.5 miles (2.4 kilometers). Although he helped work on developing the V-2 flying bomb, von Braun did not approve of the military use of the rocket. He surrendered to the Americans in 1945 and began working on rocket development for them. He was mainly responsible for the development of the first American satellite (*Explorer I*) in 1958, and for the *Saturn* rocket that took American astronauts to the Moon in 1969.

Destroying the Myths

This 1930s storybook shows invaders from Sirius trying to steal the Earth.

Ever since humans have walked on Earth, they have stared up at space and wondered what is out there. By 1959, rapidly improving technology and the desire to win the **Cold War** meant that we were nearly prepared to send people into space. But what would we find there?

There are many interesting myths about what space is. For example, if you look closely at a full moon, it appears to have a face on it. This has led some superstitious people to believe in a "man in the moon."

The Martians have landed

Other equally fanciful ideas exist about other planets and stars. Many books and films have appeared in which Martians with deadly ray guns land on Earth and begin attacking "Earthlings." Perhaps the most famous was *War of the Worlds,* written in 1898 by H.G. Wells. It gives an account of Martians landing on Earth and capturing people to drink their blood. When the story was broadcast on American radio in the 1930s, it caused widespread panic because some people thought they were listening to a real account of a Martian invasion!

Is there anybody out there?

Some people are convinced that the Unidentified Flying Objects (UFOs) seen in our skies are spaceships from other planets. Others try to explain man-made structures from our past by suggesting that there must have been help from outer space. How else could ancient peoples have built Stonehenge, or the cliff settlements at Mesa Verde in Colorado? Those who think Earth has been visited from afar point to evidence such as cave drawings that seem to have astronauts in them. Is there a simple explanation for this?

So far, our explorations into space have produced no evidence of life on other planets. Perhaps one day they will, but there is one thing of which we can be fairly sure. If we ever do find life in space, it probably won't look like a strange human being, carrying a deadly ray gun.

Does this prehistoric painting from an Italian cave show that our ancestors were visited by people in helmets with antennae?

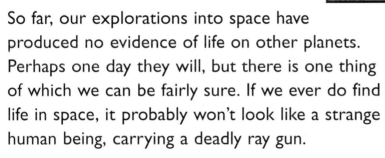

MARTIANS, AS DESCRIBED BY H.G. WELLS IN *WAR OF THE WORLDS*

"They had huge round bodies—or rather heads—about four feet in diameter, each body having in front of it a face. This face had no nostrils—indeed the Martians do not seem to have had any sense of smell—but it had a pair of very large, dark coloured eyes, and just beneath this, a kind of fleshy beak. In a group around the mouth were sixteen, slender, almost whip-like tentacles, arranged in two bunches of eight each."

Men on the Moon

From the late 1950s on, the United States and the **Soviet Union** worked tirelessly to be first to put men into space. On April 12, 1961, those working on the American space program heard the news they had been dreading. The Soviet Union had launched a manned flight. Yuri Gagarin became the first person in space. His cry of "We're off!" as his **rocket** took off became as famous in the Soviet Union as did Neil Armstrong's later words in the United States. Gagarin, the son of a carpenter, became a great Soviet hero.

The United States president, John F. Kennedy, sent a message of congratulation to the Soviet leader, Nikita Khrushchev, but really he was disappointed and felt his nation had been humiliated. He was determined that the United States would be first to achieve the next big goal in space—landing men on the Moon. A few weeks after Gagarin's flight, Kennedy made a speech in which he said, "I believe that this nation should commit itself to achieving the goal, before this decade is out, of landing a man on the Moon and returning him safely to Earth."

Yuri Gagarin was the first man in space. In April 1961, he spent 1 hour and 48 minutes **orbiting** Earth at a maximum speed of 17,000 mph (27,000 kph), or about ten times faster than a rifle bullet flies!

Into orbit

In February 1962, John Glenn became the first American to orbit Earth. For the next seven years, the space race continued. When the Soviets carried out a **spacewalk** in March 1965, the United States followed three months later. When an unmanned Soviet spacecraft landed on the Moon in February 1966, the United States was just four months behind.

But it was to be the United States that finally won the race in July 1969, when Armstrong, Aldrin, and Collins made their famous expedition. A fascinated world watched on television as mankind finally conquered the "last frontier." We had reached the Moon.

The Saturn V rocket that carried *Apollo 11* into space takes off.

SENDING *APOLLO 11* TO THE MOON

The kind of rocket that sent *Apollo 11* was called a Saturn V. It was over 360 feet (110 meters) high and weighed more than 3,300 tons, although most of this weight was fuel. The rocket was made up of three "stages."

- **Stage 1:** It fired for 2.5 minutes and enabled the rocket to reach a speed of almost 6,000 mph (9,600 kph). At about 36 miles (58 kilometers), this stage fell away into the ocean.
- **Stage 2:** The rocket was now much lighter. When the Stage 2 rockets fired for six minutes, Saturn reached a speed of about 15,500 mph (25,000 kph). At 112 miles (180 km), Stage 2 dropped away.
- **Stage 3:** These rockets fired for two minutes to reach a speed of 17,400 mph (28,000 kph)—any less, and **gravity** would have brought Saturn back to Earth. After orbiting Earth, Saturn's rockets fired again for about six minutes and sent *Apollo 11* across space to the Moon at a speed of nearly 25,000 mph (40,000 kph).

Exploring the Moon

Neil Armstrong and Buzz Aldrin are the most famous men to have set foot on the Moon, but they are not the only ones. Between 1969 and 1972, five more *Apollo* missions made the journey to the Moon successfully, and ten more men walked on its surface. All of them were from the United States.

On the last three missions, the astronauts drove around the Moon in a battery-powered car called the Lunar Rover. It allowed them to travel much further and explore more rugged terrain.

Why go back?

When the United States landed the first men on the Moon, they had won the space race. Surely that was enough. Why did they go back for so many more *Apollo* missions? The technology, money, and plans were still in place, and the astronauts wanted to go. But the most important reason was science. The *Apollo 11* astronauts had brought some soil and rock samples back with them, but scientists needed more information to answer questions, such as how and when had the Moon been formed?

On the Moon

The five *Apollo* missions that followed all landed at different sites on the Moon. Astronauts explored and mapped the Moon's mountains, valleys, and plains, although the *Apollo 14* men almost got lost in the unfamiliar lunar landscape. Astronauts set up automatic scientific stations and brought about 850 pounds (385 kilograms) of soil and rock samples back to Earth. On the last mission, *Apollo 17*, astronauts camped out on the Moon for three days.

Why stop?

The main reason the United States stopped sending men to the Moon was cost. Some people thought that the approximately $25 billion spent on the *Apollo* project might have been better spent on other things. When *Apollo 17* took off from the Moon's surface on December 14, 1972, human beings said goodbye to their closest neighbor for the last time in the twentieth century. They left a plaque behind that said, *"Here man completed his first explorations of the moon."* When, if ever, will people return?

Scientists are still studying the rock samples brought back from the moon landings that took place between 1969 and 1972.

What did they find out?

The scientists who studied the moon rocks made some exciting discoveries. They found out that the Moon is over four billion years old—about the same age as Earth. We still do not know for certain how the Moon was formed, but some scientists believe that a huge lump of rock about the size of Mars crashed into Earth over four billion years ago. This collision sent a large chunk, equal to about one-sixth of the newly formed Earth, flying off into space. The debris from the collision started to **orbit** Earth, and gradually joined together to form the Moon. The crash left a huge hole in Earth's surface that is still visible today—the basin of the Pacific Ocean.

Danger!

A journey into space is incredibly dangerous. At the moment of lift-off, astronauts are surrounded by thousands of tons of highly explosive **rocket** fuel. Once the astronauts are out in space, they have to hope that the engineers and scientists have gotten everything right. If any piece of the highly advanced technology fails, there is no emergency response team to call to come and rescue them! Fortunately, most space missions are completed without major problems, but both the Americans and the Soviets have had two fatal accidents.

Lost in space

In 1967, three American astronauts were killed a month before their *Apollo 1* was due to take off, when a spark in their cabin set fire to their spacecraft during a practice session on the launchpad.

In the same year, a Soviet **cosmonaut** died at the end of his space mission when his *Soyuz 1* spacecraft plunged to the ground in a field near Orenberg, in Russia. The parachute should have acted as a brake to slow the spacecraft down, but had become tangled and didn't open correctly.

The *Challenger* space badge includes an apple for teacher Christa McAuliffe.

In 1971, the three crew members of the Soviet *Soyuz 11* were killed when a valve failed during their **reentry** into Earth's **atmosphere.** They were not wearing pressure suits, and died as a result of **decompression sickness.** Because of the rapid change in pressure, their blood literally boiled in their veins.

The *Challenger* disaster

The most serious accident occurred in 1986. The United States had developed a reusable space "shuttle" that could be launched into space and then fly astronauts back to Earth, landing on an airstrip instead of ditching in the sea. Millions of people were watching as a huge rocket lifted the space shuttle *Challenger* towards Earth's **orbit.** On board were seven astronauts, including teacher Christa McAuliffe, the first nonprofessional astronaut to travel in space. She was to carry out experiments suggested by schoolchildren, and even hold some "live lessons" during the flight. To mark the event, an "apple for the teacher" was included in the crew's space badge.

At lift-off, a fault in one of the rocket boosters caused *Challenger* to explode just 73 seconds into its flight. Several weeks later, the remains of *Challenger* were found in the Atlantic Ocean. Investigations showed that the crew had probably survived the explosion but had been killed when the shuttle hit the sea. Mercifully, they would have fainted after just a few seconds as *Challenger* plummeted from a height of over 11 miles (18 kilometers).

The *Challenger* disaster was such a terrible shock that it was more than two and a half years before shuttle flights started again. Humankind had received a terrible reminder of the dangers of space flight.

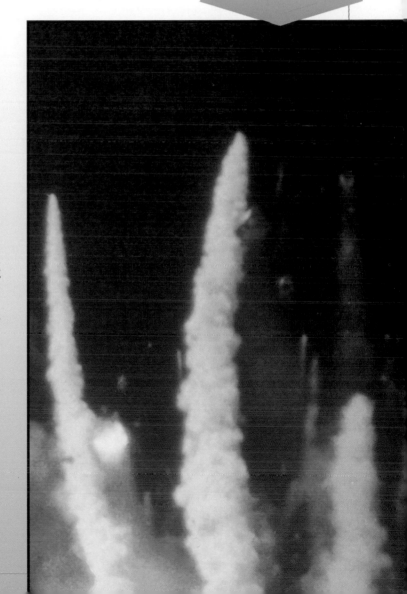

The space shuttle *Challenger* exploded only 73 seconds after it lifted off on January 28, 1986.

Beyond the Moon

By 1981, people had made six visits to the Moon, and had perfected a space shuttle that could be used over and over again. It seemed that humankind was close to conquering space. Steps were already under way to learn about the universe far beyond. In fact, long before *Apollo 11* reached the Moon, spacecraft had been sent deep into that universe. By the end of the twentieth century, space **probes** had visited every planet except distant Pluto.

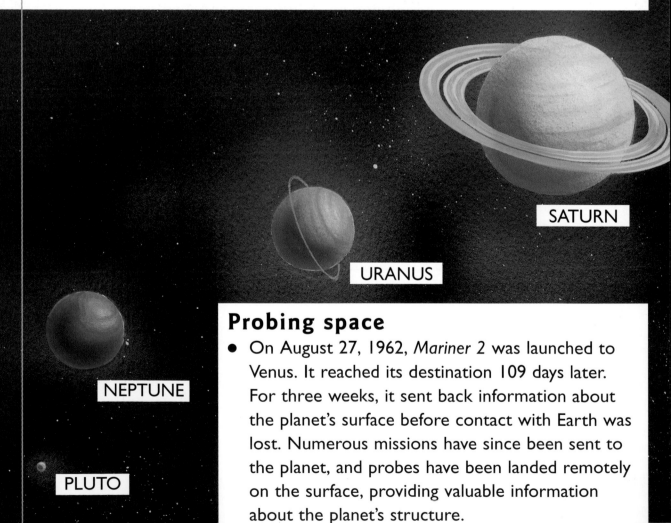

SATURN

URANUS

NEPTUNE

PLUTO

Probing space

- On August 27, 1962, *Mariner 2* was launched to Venus. It reached its destination 109 days later. For three weeks, it sent back information about the planet's surface before contact with Earth was lost. Numerous missions have since been sent to the planet, and probes have been landed remotely on the surface, providing valuable information about the planet's structure.

- In July 1965, *Mariner 4* sent back the first close-up pictures of Mars. By 1971, further missions had mapped the planet's whole surface. In 1989, U.S. President George Bush set a target of a manned landing on Mars by the year 2019. Scientists still have a long way to go before the three-year round trip can be undertaken. For example, in 1999, a Mars probe was lost when the multinational developers failed to allow for the difference between metric and imperial measurements in calculating its course.

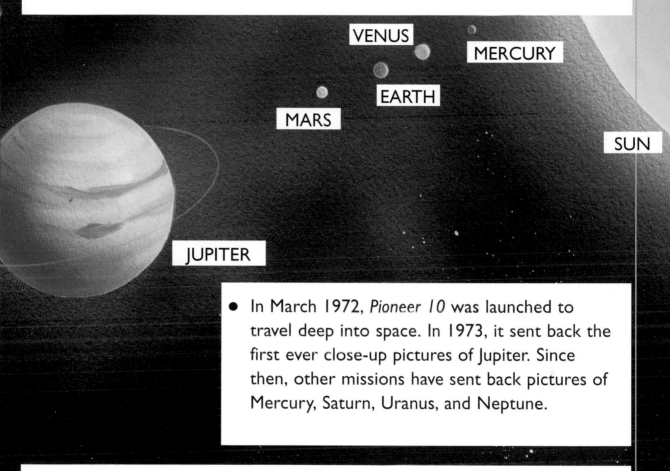

- In March 1972, *Pioneer 10* was launched to travel deep into space. In 1973, it sent back the first ever close-up pictures of Jupiter. Since then, other missions have sent back pictures of Mercury, Saturn, Uranus, and Neptune.

Living in space

As our knowledge of our universe increases, the day when humans may live in space, or in colonies on other planets, gets closer. Both the Americans and the Soviets have launched **space stations,** which can be used to test the effects on the human body of spending long periods in space. In 1986, the **Soviet Union** launched the space station *Mir,* and two astronauts stayed on it for a whole year. Since then, it has been used by many astronauts from around the world. The U.S., Russia, and fourteen other countries are now building a new international space station, to be completed in 2004.

Space Facts

Taking off

Within four seconds of lift-off, the space shuttle reaches a speed of 100 miles per hour (160 kilometers per hour). Within 40 seconds, it is traveling at more than the speed of sound. The pressure that astronauts experience during this acceleration is about ten times that felt by airline passengers during takeoff. After 8.5 minutes, the engines cut off as the shuttle leaves the Earth's **atmosphere.** Some astronauts cheer at this point, as the terrible pressure on their bodies is replaced by **weightlessness.**

During lift-off, there is a danger that the shuttle might lose control. In case this happens, spacecraft are fitted with a flight termination system (FTS). If there were a danger that an out-of-control shuttle might threaten life on Earth, a member of the space team on the ground would send a signal and the craft would blow up. Inevitably, the crew would be killed.

A basic question

Astronauts complain that when they give interviews, the question that everyone wants to ask is, "How do you go to the bathroom in space?" Spacecraft do have toilets, but they are flushed by air, because water does not flow in space. It has been described as like "going to the bathroom in a vacuum cleaner." Solid waste is carried back to Earth, but liquid waste is dumped in space. One astronaut described the "urine dump" as beautiful to watch because the fluid instantly turns into shiny ice crystals.

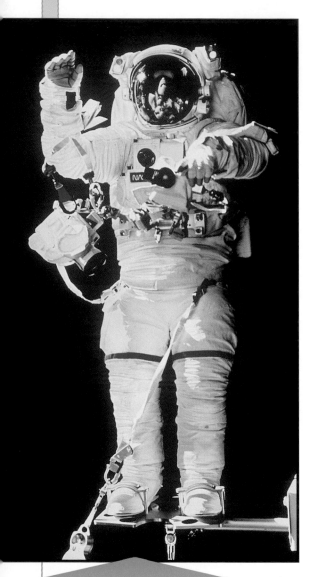

An astronaut's spacesuit enables him or her to survive the hostile environment outside the spacecraft.

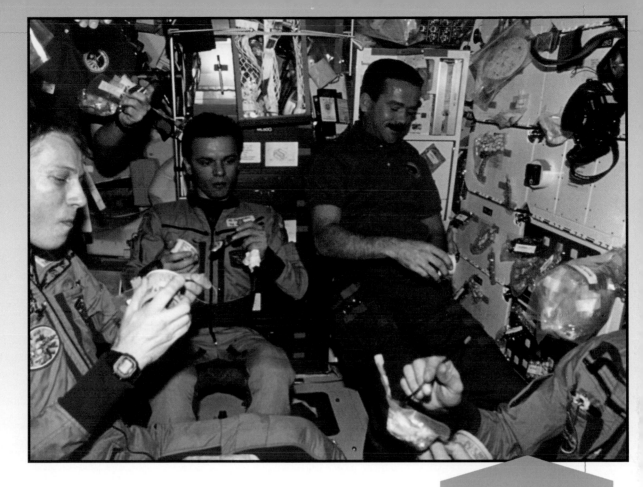

Weightlessness

Once in space, there is no **gravity,** and anything that is not tied down floats. If you cut yourself in this weightless environment, the blood forms a perfectly spherical droplet and floats away like a tiny red balloon. Astronauts sleep in sleeping bags attached to the wall. This keeps them from banging into each other. It also means that when they go to sleep, they can wake up in the same place.

Astronauts look fatter in space than on Earth, because more blood than usual goes to the head. If they lived in space for long periods, they would get taller, because there is no gravity to compact their bones. In a weightless environment, muscles do hardly any work. Exercise is important to keep these muscles from turning into flab.

It is hard to eat in a weightless environment. Food packages must be designed to keep the food from floating away.

What Have We Gained from the Space Race?

Space exploration is incredibly expensive. For example, between 1969 and 1972, the *Apollo* project cost the United States over $25 billion. Some critics of space flight have suggested that the money would be better spent on fighting poverty or famine. When the **Soviet Union** broke up into its individual states in 1991, its space program virtually came to an end because it was so expensive. So has it all been worth it?

Does it really cost so much?

The National Aeronautics and Space Administration (NASA), which runs the United States space program, argues that space exploration is not really expensive. It says that thousands of jobs have been created by the space race and that advances in technology brought about through space exploration have made United States businesses more efficient and profitable. It calculates that, for every $1 spent on the space program, the U.S. has become richer by $7, because of extra taxes paid by space program workers, or from improvements in the economy. Whether or not NASA is correct, the space race has definitely brought enormous benefits.

This is NASA ground control in Houston, from where space flights are managed.

Advances in science and technology

To put people on the Moon, scientists have had to overcome some very difficult problems.

- How do we get outside Earth's **atmosphere?**
- How do we keep spacecraft from burning up on **reentry?**
- How do we communicate with astronauts in space?
- How do we cope with **weightlessness?**

In finding solutions to these problems, the teams working on the space program have vastly increased our knowledge of science and technology.

Satellite communications

These scientific and technological advances have provided many benefits for people in general, outside the space program. **Satellites** in **orbit** above the earth are used to relay television pictures, to speed up intercontinental telephone calls, and to provide valuable information about the earth. Details of extreme weather, such as hurricanes, can be identified by satellites. The existence of a huge hole in the **ozone layer** over the Antarctic was confirmed by the satellite *Nimbus 7* in 1987. In 1999, the United States launched the satellite *Ikonos*. It provides pictures of the earth that are so detailed that they can pick out objects on the ground as small as three feet (one meter) across.

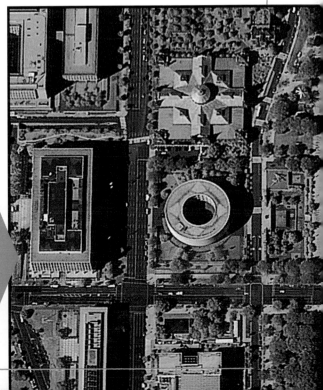

This is part of New York City as viewed from space. It is now possible to download images that have been sent from satellites onto any computer within minutes.

Spin-offs

The increased scientific and technological developments needed to overcome the problems involved in space travel have produced **spin-offs** that have improved everyday life on Earth.

Medicine

One of the areas to see major benefits has been medicine. In 1990, the Hubble Space Telescope was launched to give better views of space. The same technology is now used to help doctors find cancer in sick people. Since devices used in spacecraft have to be very small and light, many tiny instruments have become available to doctors and surgeons. For example, a television camera the size of an audio cassette can be attached to a surgeon's head to give students and other surgeons close-up views of operations. There are hearing aids smaller than a human fingernail, and wheelchairs that can be steered by voice controls, just as astronauts sometimes have to steer spacecraft by voice.

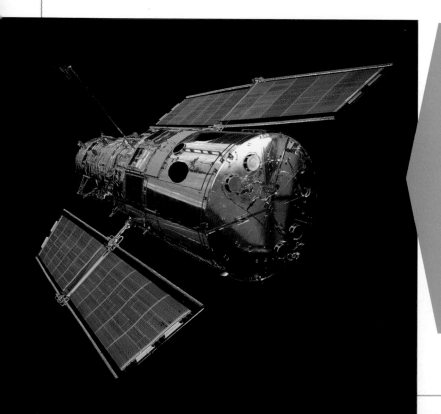

The Hubble Space Telescope, in **orbit** around Earth at a height of 380 miles (610 kilometers), has no crew. From outside Earth's **atmosphere,** it takes images of space that are better than pictures produced through any land-based telescope.

There have been other valuable nonelectronic spin-offs in medicine. The insulating material used for **rocket** fuel tanks can be used in hospitals to prevent bedsores. Aerospace engineers have also produced a special bed that allows patients with serious burns to float more comfortably on a cushion of air.

Daily life

Daily life has been affected by the space program, maybe more than anyone realizes. The need for small but powerful instruments on board spacecraft led to the invention of the silicon chip—the tiny electronic circuit-board that is an essential part of every computer today. Cars are designed by a computer program first made to design spaceships. Wristwatches run on tiny batteries designed to time devices in space.

Even training shoes are products of the space program. The need to develop moonboots, with cushioning and ventilation, has resulted in better footwear for athletes, which reduces fatigue and the chances of injury.

SPACE IN THE KITCHEN
Did you know that non-stick frying pans and casserole dishes that can go straight from the freezer to the oven, and then on to your table, are the result of the space program? Spacecraft go through extremes of heat in space, and materials had to be developed that could resist these temperatures. Now they are used to make your kitchenware!

Space Exploration— Building a Better Future?

From conflict to cooperation

One of the key driving forces behind the space race was the desire to prove the supremacy of Western culture and technology over that of Eastern Europe, or vice versa. In December 1989, the United States and the **Soviet Union** announced that the **Cold War** was over. International conflict could be replaced with international cooperation. In fact, as early as 1975, Soviet and American teams had worked together on a joint *Apollo–Soyuz* mission. Since 1989, they have cooperated on developing the Soviet **space station,** *Mir,* which has regular visits from Russian, American, and West European astronauts. In 1996, the giant U.S. soft drink company, Pepsi, became the first company to produce an advertisement in space, when *Mir* astronauts filmed a huge model Pepsi can 200 miles (320 kilometers) above the earth.

EXPLORING THE UNIVERSE—WHAT NEXT?

Earth is not the only planet in the universe, and humans may not be the only living organisms. Space exploration enables us to find out more about the Sun, the Moon, and the planets. In time, we may even be able to visit other **solar systems.**

We have discovered that the Moon is not made of cheese, as some people once thought. However, there is every chance that valuable minerals will be found on the Moon or the planets—or that new minerals will be discovered.

As Earth's population increases, we are beginning to run out of living space. Space exploration may provide a possible solution. The time when space cities can be built to house thousands of people, either on the Moon or floating in space, may not be too far away. With a controlled climate and specially built houses and areas for growing food, these might be very desirable places to live.

A turning point?

In many ways, the moon landing was a turning point in our history. The great challenge of taking people to another part of our universe, and bringing them back, had been achieved. Now we can look toward international space stations, such as that being built by the United States and fifteen other countries. Space cities and visits to other planets are no longer just dreams. The fact that it was the United States that first put men on the Moon may also have made the moon landing a turning point in the Cold War, as the U.S. came to dominate the space race in the 1980s. Gradually, the Soviet influence in Europe decreased, and the Cold War was formally declared over in December 1989.

Some people argue that the real turning point was in 1957, when the Soviet Union put a **rocket** into space. Perhaps the moon landing—and the type of space program we have today, with its emphasis on unmanned flights to distant planets—grew from the breakthrough in 1957. It is up to each of us to make up our own minds.

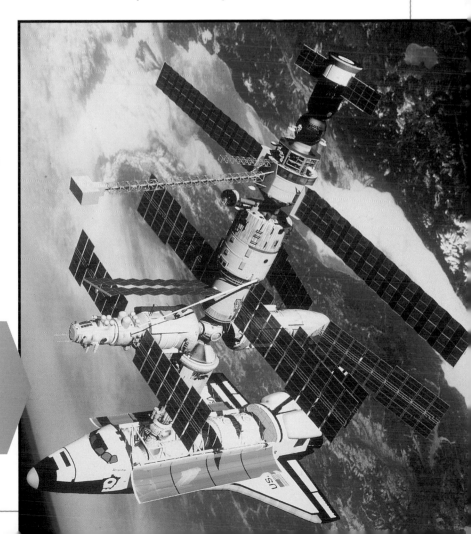

The shuttle and *Mir* space station **orbit** the earth.

Important Dates

1783	September	Montgolfier brothers launch hot-air balloon
1903	December	First flight of manned aircraft by Wright brothers
1941		Sir Frank Whittle invents the **jet engine**
1945	August	**Atomic bombs** dropped on Hiroshima and Nagasaki
1952		World's first jetliner goes into service
1957	October 4	USSR launches *Sputnik 1*
1957	November	USSR launches *Sputnik 2*, with dog on board
1958	January	Launch of American *Explorer 1*
1959		United States sends monkeys into space
1961	April 12	Yuri Gagarin is the first man in space
1962	February	John Glenn is the first American to **orbit** the earth
1962	August 27	*Mariner 2* **probe** takes off for Venus
1964	November	*Mariner 4* probe takes off for Mars
1965	March	First **spacewalk**
1967	January	*Apollo 1* catches fire on launchpad
1967	April	*Soyuz 1* crashes on **reentry**
1969	July 20	*Apollo 11* lands on the Moon
1969	November	*Apollo 12* astronauts spend nearly 32 hours on moon
1971	February	*Apollo 14* astronauts nearly get lost on lunar highlands
1971	June	*Soyuz 11* **cosmonauts** die from **decompression sickness**
1971	July	Lunar Rover used for first time
1972	March	*Pioneer 10* takes off for Jupiter
1972	December	*Apollo 17* is the last manned spacecraft to land on the Moon
1986	January 28	*Challenger* space shuttle explodes
1986	February 20	**Space station** *Mir* launched
1987		*Nimbus 7* **satellite** confirms the existence of a hole in the **ozone layer** over the Antarctic
1989	December	End of the **Cold War**
1990	April	Hubble Space Telescope launched
1999		Satellite *Ikonos* sends back highly detailed pictures of Earth

Glossary

atmosphere band of gases surrounding Earth or another planet

atomic bomb weapon that gets its explosive force from the splitting of atoms of a substance such as uranium or plutonium

Cold War dispute between Western countries and Eastern Europe after World War II

command module main part of the spacecraft that orbited above the Moon; during moon landings, the lunar module separated from it to descend to the Moon's surface

communist person or state that follows communism, a classless society in which land and industry are owned by the state, and profits are used for the good of the people; personal freedom and enterprise are limited

cosmonaut Soviet astronaut

decompression sickness painful medical condition when nitrogen bubbles form in the blood as a result of rapid changes in pressure

democratic type of government in which leaders are elected by the people

gravity force exerted by a large object, such as a planet, that pulls smaller objects toward it

ICBM intercontinental ballistic missile— nuclear missile that can travel a great distance

jet engine powerful engine that uses gas to gain forward thrust

lunar module part of the spacecraft that separated from the command module and carried astronauts to the surface of the Moon

nuclear bomb bomb that gets its explosive force from the joining of atoms of the gases hydrogen and helium

orbit circle around a planet above its atmosphere, or to travel along such a path

ozone layer layer of gas in Earth's atmosphere that reduces the strong effects of the Sun's radiation

probe unmanned spacecraft sent to find out about other regions of space

reentry return of a spacecraft to Earth's atmosphere from space

rocket engine that moves forward by pushing gases out behind it

satellite small object sent into orbit around a planet

solar system system of planets that move in orbit around a sun

Soviet Union former collection of states in Eastern Europe, led by Russia; also called the USSR

space station spacecraft "parked" in space to act as a base

spacewalk travel by an astronaut outside a spacecraft while in space

spin-off product developed as a result of technological developments

superpower name given to the U.S. and Soviet Union after World War II

weightlessness being in a place where there is no gravity; nothing keeps you on the ground and you float in space freely

More Books to Read

Gold, Susan D. *Countdown to the Moon*. Parsippany, N.J.: Silver Burdett Press, 1992.

Green, Jen. *Race to the Moon: The Story of Apollo 11*. Danbury, Conn.: Franklin Watts, 1998.

Kallen, Stuart A. *The Race to Space*. Edina, Minn.: ABDO Publishing Company, 1996.

Index